Self-Love

A Guide to Loving Yourself Unapologetically

TAMIKO LOWRY PUGH

SS | **Still Standing**
Publishing Company

OTHER BOOKS BY
TAMIKO LOWRY-PUGH

Wounds To Wisdom...I'm Still Standing

Wounds To Wisdom...The Survivor Series

The Empowerment Formula: 6 Steps For
Living An Empowered Life!

Tamiko Lowry-Pugh

Dedication

This book is dedicated to all of the self-love ambassadors of the world who believe in the power of self-love.

Contents

Love yourself for who you really are because God created you to be unique, rare, one-of-a-kind, valuable and precious.

Introduction

When most of us think about love, most often we think about the love we give others or the love we feel for other. But what about the love we give ourselves? Self-love is the foundation where love for others begins and ends.

The most important decision of your life, the one that will affect every other decision you make, is the commitment to love and accept yourself. It directly affects the quality of your relationships, your work, your free time, your faith, and your future.

Over the course of the next 21 days. I encourage you to give yourself the gift of self-love by making a commitment to do something loving for you; no matter how big or small every day for 21 days. When you treat yourself with kindness, it makes you feel good. The more you feel good, the more you want to treat yourself with kindness. Each loving act, no matter how big or small is a brick in the foundation of self-love.

This book guide you in the area of self-love and how to love yourself from the inside out unapologetically by providing you with self-love tips, affirmations, and mantras that you can use to assist you in the 21 days of Self-Love.

Take some time to do something loving for you. You deserve it!

You must love yourself before you love another. By accepting yourself and fully being what you are, your simple presence can make others happy.

5 signs that you lack self-love

1. You are settling in your less than your heart and soul deserve. You are playing small. Letting fear stagnate you. Sacrificing your dreams. Procrastinating. Listening to conventional wisdom instead of going for the life your heart and soul craves. AFFIRM: I never settle for less than my heart and soul desire.

2. You are in relationships that don't support you or fully honor you. You are in relationships that drain you or degrade you, dishonor you in any way. You hold on to friends, lovers, clients that aren't supporting you to grow or be your best self. AFFIRM: I have loving and respectful relationships.

3. You're always being hard on yourself. You criticize instead of appreciating yourself. You put unnecessary pressure on yourself. AFFIRM: I am always gentle, kind and compassionate with myself.

4. You treat your body poorly by neglecting and demeaning it, instead of adoring it or treating it like a temple. AFFIRM: I always treat my body like a sacred temple.

5. You sacrifice what you really want and need, giving more than you have to give. AFFIRM: I always stay true to myself.

yourself

Begin your day with love.
Remind yourself of your
worthiness before getting out
of bed. Breathe in love

Day 1
Raise Your
Awareness

Begin to pay attention to how you treat yourself compared to how you treat your friends and family members. Are you treating others better than you treat yourself? Most self-love blocks are habits that you can break when you become aware of them. Habits are those automatic responses you use to respond to situations. You have the power to hurt yourself or make yourself feel good. What's your choice?

- ➤ To beat yourself up for a mistake or forgive yourself?
- ➤ To take mean things that people say personally or refuse to give them power?
- ➤ To stay in an unhappy relationship

because you're scared of being alone or to walk away because you deserve better?

➤ To be a Doormat and ignore your own needs or to set boundaries so that your needs are met?

Self-love helps you make better choices that are in your own best interest. Most of the time the choices that you make are based on choices you've made in the past. Pay attention and start to think before you react in a negative situation. Try to take a more loving approach. If you keep your awareness high, you will eventually create healthier, loving habits.

DAY 1 ASSIGNMENT

Write down 3 ways that you can begin to create healthier loving habits.

DAY 1 AFFIRMATION

I will raise my awareness and create healthier loving habits!

Day 2
Look For Love
In The Right
Places

We often look for love from a romantic partner, friends, and family and then complain when we don't feel loved. We chase love in many directions yet rarely feel fulfilled. Please understand that being loved begins and ends with you! It's hard to receive love if you don't love yourself. People can say, "I love you," and do nice things for you all day every day. But, if you don't love yourself, it still won't make you feel content inside on a long-term basis.

If you want love in your life, go to the mirror RIGHT NOW! And say, "I will make an effort to be more loving to you, starting today!" Say it with feeling. It will raise your awareness as it relates to doing loving things for yourself. Find the love inside you. It's there!

DAY 2 ASSIGNMENT

Write down 3 things you love about yourself.

DAY 2 AFFIRMATION

I will look for love in the right places starting with me!

Day 3 Change to Loving Responses

Begin making an effort to find new ways to respond to situations that bring you down. If someone makes a negative comment about you, smile and say "thank you" and then affirm to yourself, "I love and accept myself as I am." Responding from a place of self-love instead of feeling deeply wounded takes some of the sting out of their words. The more you do this; your reaction to negative comments will get better. And people will less likely take jabs at you.

It takes time to break lifetime habits. For now, begin to raise your self-awareness.

Just become more aware of the things you say or do out of habit that keep you feeling down about yourself. Don't get angry or upset with yourself. We all do things that aren't in our own best interest because of insecurities and the need for people to like us. Pay attention gently, lovingly, and without any criticism.

DAY 3 ASSIGNMENT

Make a list composed of all of your goodness, then hang it where you can see it daily.

DAY 3 AFFIRMATION

I will respond to negativity from a place of love.

Day 4

Accept

Compliments

Graciously

Most of us were taught that being modest will make people like us more. When you don't love yourself, it can be difficult to receive a compliment and believe it. Being too modest can make you deflect kind words or even deny your assets. "No, I didn't lose weight. It must be the light." When you don't love yourself, it's hard to accept kind words. Even if you have to consciously force yourself, in the beginning, practice receiving compliments graciously. When you get compliments, practice saying "thank you," be quiet, and allow yourself to feel special. You deserve it!

DAY 4 ASSIGNMENT

Fill in the blank.

Something that makes me unique is...

DAY 4 AFFIRMATION

I accept compliments graciously because
I deserve it.

Day 5

Be Your Real Best Friend

Think about what you would say to your best friend who broke something or said the wrong thing or made a big mistake. You would probably do your best to reassure them that everything was OK! Next time you do something that you regret, think about what you would say to a friend who did the same thing.

Would you yell at them or console them? Call her names or be kind? Hold a grudge for a long time or forgive them? You know you would make the latter choice in most cases. Get into the habit of stopping yourself from reacting negatively and treat yourself the way you would treat your friend.

DAY 5 ASSIGNMENT

Why do you treat your best friend better than you treat yourself? In what ways can you begin to treat yourself like you would treat your best friend?

DAY 5 AFFIRMATION

I am my real best friend, and I treat myself with love. I love myself; therefore I live totally in the now, experiencing each moment as good and knowing that my future is bright, joyous and secure. For I am a beloved child of God and He lovingly takes care of me now and forever more.

Day 6

Redefine Your

Self-Image

Stop focusing on what you're not and pay more attention to the beautiful person you are. Instead of looking for what's wrong with you, find your good qualities and appreciate them. Let those good qualities define you, instead of what you don't have.

Not being thin doesn't mean you're fat! Not having a degree doesn't make you dumb. Not being the fastest doesn't make you slow. Accepting this will increase your self-love and confidence. Comparing yourself to others will block self- love since you can always find someone who makes you fall short and feel like you're lacking.

What you're not doesn't make you what you are. Love yourself for who you really are because God created you to be a unique, rare, one-of-a-kind, valuable and precious woman.

DAY 6 ASSIGNMENT

Think about 5 fantastic attributes you inherited from your parents. If you never knew your parents or your relationship with them is an unhappy one, who influenced you? Make a list of 5 important things they taught you, that have impacted the way you live your life today.

DAY 6 AFFIRMATION

I love myself for who I am because
I am enough!

Day 7 Say "I Love Me" As Often As Possible

Unfortunately, many of us are not brought up to say "I love me." It can feel strange and funny at first. It will continue to feel that way for a while. Go to a mirror right now! Look into it, and say, "I love you" to your reflection. The more you say it, the more you remind yourself that you want to feel self-love. The more you say it, the more it will sink in. The more you say it, the more you will fall in love with you.

Falling in love with yourself takes time and patience. As you continue to do it, it will begin to feel more natural. You'll get more comfortable with it. Think of it as practice for real love one day. Say "I love you," every single time you pass a mirror. It's a lovely day when you say "I love me" and realize that it's true! Practice makes perfect, and then it turns into real genuine love!

DAY 7 ASSIGNMENT

Wake up every morning on a thankful note. Hug yourself and give a pat on your shoulder. There is Japanese concept called the 'ikigai' – it is a simple reason that you want to wake up every day, a reason for being. It is said that finding it requires deep soul searching. But I feel, it can be found in simple things. Celebrate your health, your sexuality, your body, your talents, your passions, develop a new relationship with yourself. Thank yourself often and enough.

DAY 7 AFFIRMATION

I deeply love and approve of myself. I am a
perfect reflection of my beautiful soul.
I love me!

Day 8

Accept Your Body

You don't have to be happy with every inch of your body to love and accept it. Stressing out over how your body looks sends a message that you disapprove of you. That is not loving to you! Many people say they're happy with how they look. Yet they all have wonderful qualities they overlook because of their disapproval for something about their bodies. All the plastic surgery and body tweaking going on for celebrities sets standards that the average person can't attain.

Instead of accepting it, we obsess over the flaws we see or the weight we can't seem to lose. This is negative energy! Unconditional self-love means loving all of you, despite your flaws. It's OK to want to do what you can to look your best. Try to be as fit and healthy as possible by working out and eating healthy without stressing over being "the media's" version of perfect. It's loving to want to feel as good as possible. It's not loving to postpone self-acceptance until your body is as perfect as you imagine it could be. You may never love yourself if you do.

DAY 8 ASSIGNMENT

Change your inner dialogue. It's been said that we teach others how to treat us. If we believe that, the message that comes across to others is that we are not worth being liked, loved, or treated with respect. Most of it comes from what we're not even saying. Choose to believe that you have the right to be respected and treated with dignity and act like it! List 3 ways you can begin to change your inner dialogue. Start implementing it immediately.

DAY 8 AFFIRMATION

I love myself! Therefore, I take loving care of my body. I lovingly feed it nourishing foods and beverages, I lovingly groom it and dress it, and my body lovingly responds to me with vibrant health and energy. I love every part of my body, flaws and all.

Day 9
Schedule A
"Me Day"

People who with little self-love rarely have time for themselves and the activities they enjoy because they're so fixed on doing what others want. Or just don't make time for themselves. This is very unloving! "ME time" is essential for your happiness and emotional well-being. Every time you make a little time to do something just for you is a lovely act of self-love. Try taking "ME time" to the next level!

Schedule a "ME day"—a whole day that's ALL about YOU—to say a big loud "I love me!" Go to your calendar right now! And choose a day that will work for you. A whole entire day! Weekends can be easier, but it's also fun to take a day off from work to play. No chores or errands. Just for things you enjoy. Plan your day ahead of time. Think about what you would like to do. Write it down and look forward to it. Don't tell anyone your plans, unless it's someone you trust to be happy for you.

DAY 9 ASSIGNMENT

Write down a list of 5 things that you can do as "me time," and add them to your calendar.

DAY 9 AFFIRMATION

I make time for me because I love me and I deserve it! I love myself before I love another. By accepting myself and fully being who I am, my simple presence can make others happy.

Day 10
Listen To Your
Inner Dialogue

What's really running through your mind? What are you thinking and saying to yourself? Are you speaking words of love, power, possibility and success? Or are you chattering in fear, doubt, and scarcity? When you are aware of the quality of your thoughts and consciously decide to raise them, you find you become gentler with yourself. Remember, Life and death are in the power of the tongue. From this day forward begin to speak life over yourself and every situation.

DAY 10 ASSIGNMENT

Begin to speak life over yourself by repeating the following affirmations every day for the next 21 days while looking in the mirror.

DAY 10 AFFIRMATIONS

I speak and think positive words of love and success over my life every day.

I matter

I am loved

I can make it

I am blessed

I am a winner

I am strong

I am healed

I am whole

I can do this

Yes I can

Day 11

Be

Spontaneous!

Look for ways to be more spontaneous. If you're doing chores and look out the window staring at the sunshine, go for a long walk or call a friend to do something outdoors. If you have extra time off from work, see if there are last minute deals for a quick vacation. Everything you do will enrich your life in some way, whether you have fun or learn a lesson and get to know someone better or try something you want to do again.

Being spontaneous loosens you up, so to speak, by making you more flexible about how you live. Being flexible allows you to go with the flow of life more and that flow can take you to great places. It allows you to try new things and take more risks in life. Do something last minute, or at the spur of the moment that you'd normally say no to or make excuses for why you can't. Leave the laundry for another time. Record the TV show you planned to watch. Get out and have fun! Begin to open up your life to new dimensions. When you do this, you are saying to yourself, "I love me!" Remember! YOLO (you only live once).

DAY 11 ASSIGNMENT

Make a list of 3-5 ways that you can be more spontaneous. Set a date and start doing it.

DAY 11 AFFIRMATION

I am spontaneous and flexible

Day 12

Stop Being a

Victim

Do you blame others for your unhappiness? Do you complain that you hate being a victim? Playing a victim is your choice. No one can force you to give up your personal power. People Pleasers complain about who did them wrong. It's your choice to accept behavior you don't like or to love yourself enough to change your response to it.

Relinquish self-pity and begin to change your situation! Why stay a victim? Taking a stand makes people less likely to take advantage of you. You control how people treat you. Nobody uses someone who won't allow it. And nobody is a victim unless they choose to be. Victims feel helpless, which brings self-esteem down.

You are not helpless. You always have spiritual support in uplifting yourself from living as a victim to setting boundaries and being happier. The ball is in your court. Think about what makes you feel like a victim and how you can change the situation. The more you nurture self-love, the less you will allow people to treat you poorly, and the less you will feel like a victim. Begin to take responsibility for how people treat you.

DAY 12 ASSIGNMENT

Own Your Own Life - The truth is no one can control your life because no one can control your thoughts. Suffering comes from living in the pain of the past or the fear of the future. Focus your attention on the present moment and be at peace.

DAY 12 AFFIRMATION

I now take responsibility for the way people treat me and relinquish self-pity!

Day 13
Give Yourself
Hugs

Hugs are therapeutic, even when you give them to yourself. Studies have shown that the more hugs you get, the stronger your well-being. Touch is therapeutic for your emotional health. Hugs, caressing, massages, etc. all do more than just feel good at the moment. They have lingering results. While it's nice to get hugs and caresses from others, you can provide it to you at any time! Hugging yourself says, "I love me," and helps you to feel good.

DAY 13 ASSIGNMENT

Wrap your arms around yourself for a minute when no one is around. It may feel funny the first few times, but eventually, you'll get used to it and then enjoy the benefits. Hold yourself. Rub your arms and any other parts your hand's touch. Close your eyes and appreciate how good touch feels, even if it's from you. While they are not a substitute for being hugged by someone else, they're a separate feel-good action. Have you hugged yourself yet? Give yourself a hug now!

DAY 13 AFFIRMATION

I hug myself daily because I love me!

Day 14

Meditate

Meditation helps you get into a state of relaxation. With the world going so fast, most people feel the stress of trying to keep up. Closing your eyes and breathing to a rhythm as you meditate can create space for you and build inner peace. Pushing yourself to keep up with life at the expense of your stress levels is very unloving. Meditation can bring you back to peace.

Try meditation on your own or with a group. You don't have to spend a lot of time doing it. You might not be able to sit still at first but keep going. The more you do it, the easier it is to do. Try it for a few minutes. Work your way to fifteen minutes a day. As you get more in touch with your inner self, self-love will grow.

DAY 14 ASSIGNMENT

Begin mediating for at least 5 minutes per day. You can do this by closing your eyes and reciting an affirmation or mantra. If you need help with staying focused on your meditations, there are some great guided meditations on YouTube. Or you can visit my website to download one of my guided meditation or affirmation mp3's.

DAY 14 AFFIRMATION

I meditate daily because it brings me to a state of peace and relaxation!

Day 15

Set Boundaries

I don't know the key to success, but the
key to failure is trying to please everybody
~Bill Cosby

Setting healthy boundaries opens the door
to create healthy relationships. Unhealthy
boundaries create dysfunctional ones. By
establishing clear boundaries, we define
ourselves in relation to others. To do this.
However, we must be able to identify and
respect our needs, feelings, opinions, and
rights. Otherwise, our efforts would be like
putting a fence around a yard without
knowing the property lines.

Here are some tips for setting healthy
boundaries:

When you identify the need to establish
boundaries, do it clearly, preferably without
anger, and in as few words as possible. Do
not justify, apologize, or rationalize for the

boundary you are setting. Do not argue! Just set the boundary in a calm, firm, clear and respectful way.

You can't set a boundary and take care of someone else's feelings at the same time. You are not responsible for the other person's reaction to the boundary you are setting. You are only responsible for communicating the boundary in a respectful manner. If others get upset with you, that is their problem. If they no longer want your friendship, then you are probably better off without them. You do not need "friends" who disrespect your boundaries.

At first, you will probably feel selfish, guilty, or embarrassed when you set a boundary. Do it anyway, and tell yourself you have a right to take care of yourself. Setting boundaries takes lots of practice and determination. Don't let anxiety or low self-esteem prevent you from taking care of yourself.

When you feel anger or resentment, or find yourself whining or complaining, you probably need to set a boundary. Listen to yourself, then determine what you need to do or say. Then communicate your boundary assertively. When you are confident you can set healthy boundaries with others, you will have less need to put up walls.

When you set boundaries, you might be tested, especially by those accustomed to controlling, abusing you, or manipulating you. Plan on it, expect it, but be firm. Remember, your behavior must match the boundaries you are setting. You cannot establish a clear boundary successfully if you send a mixed message by apologizing for doing so. Be firm, clear, and respectful.

Learning to set healthy boundaries takes time. It is a process. You will set boundaries when you are ready. It's your growth in your own time frame, not what someone else tells you. Let your counselor or support group help you with pace and process.

Develop a good support system of people who respect your right to set boundaries. Eliminate toxic persons from your life - those who want to manipulate you, abuse you, and control you.

Setting healthy boundaries allows your true self to emerge – and what an exciting journey that is.

DAY 15 ASSIGNMENT

Think of a place you'd like to have better boundaries. Start simple.

– Imagine yourself setting the boundary.

– What do you think the person would say? If it's distressful, tap on the reaction you imagine.

– Go back and start again.

– Keep practicing until it feels good or at least neutral, no matter how "they" might react.

DAY 15 AFFIRMATION

I understand my personal boundaries and respect the boundaries of others.

Day 16

Clear The

Clutter

Clutter is nothing more than postponed decisions ~Barbara Hemphill

This is the perfect time to begin clearing clutter for the mind, body, and soul and to get rid out what no longer serves us well. Letting go of the old, worn out or stale is a powerful action that creates new space for fresh, wonderful, new beginnings!

Begin clearing clutter by getting rid of things, people or ideas that no longer serve a purpose in our lives. For example, if you look in your pantry, you are likely to find some items that expired a long time ago. These items are not safe to eat, and you will never use them, but for some reason they remain on the shelf taking up valuable space.

Look in your closet. There are probably clothes in there that you know you will never wear again. But, year after year, they remain in your closet taking up valuable space and leaving a cluttered mess. There is also mental clutter that clogs our brains with old ideas and memories that do not serve us well.

Take a look at the people in your life. Many of them serve no purpose. They are not adding value to your life, they don't serve you well, and many of those friendships expired a long time ago. For some reason we feel the need to keep them around allowing them to take up precious, valuable space in our lives.

When we don't clear the clutter from our lives, we aren't able to let new feelings, experiences, projects, visions and those new relationships flow in. We often can become so focused on wanting to add so much more to our lives that we don't realize that what we get rid of can have the most profound impact of all.

DAY 16 ASSIGNMENT

As you begin to clear the clutter out of your life, ask yourself these questions:

* Is the clutter that meeting a specific need in my life?

* What fears do I have in letting go of the items that I don't use anymore?

* What void is the clutter filling?

* What thoughts or feelings am I avoiding by keeping the clutter around?

* What stories am I telling myself about why I can't let these things go?

Try getting to the root of the issue by understanding the role clutter is playing in your emotional life, then you can begin to find more effective ways to deal with emotional needs and begin letting the clutter go. If you are unsure of where to start, consider getting a professional life coach that specializes in clearing clutter as it relates to emotional issues. Remember, you want to let go of clutter from the inside out.

Clear the clutter so that you can let go of the past, and release old habits that hold you back and allow for new things to flow in its place.

DAY 16 AFFIRMATION

I live in a clutter-free environment, mentally, spiritually, emotionally.

Day 17

Value Yourself!

Value yourself! The only people who appreciate a doormat are people with dirty shoes! ~Anon

How much are you worth? If you don't value yourself, it's hard to attract self-love, confidence, or success. One of the best ways to show that you value yourself is to be kind to yourself. Every time you treat yourself with love, you reinforce being worthy. Self-love translates into having greater value. The more love you have, the more love you believe you deserve.

Make sure you get paid for your skills. Break any habits of giving them away to anyone who asks for a favor. The more you value you, the more other people will value you and the more confidence you will build. Throughout the day say, "Darn I'm good!" Do it in the mirror when possible. Convince yourself that you have a high value! You'll love yourself for doing it!

The truth is if we don't value ourselves, and who we are at our core, others won't value us either. We teach other people how to treat us – so it's a good idea to Value Yourself starting now!

DAY 17 ASSIGNMENT

Identify a time in life when you were happiest.

What were you doing?

Were you with other people? Who?

What other factors contributed to your happiness?

The answers to the previous questions will reveal your current values.

DAY 17 AFFIRMATION

I value myself because I know
my self-worth

Day 18:

Let Faith

Support You

Keep praying. Keep the faith. But most of all, trust that God's infinite wisdom has every solution to every situation. Self-Love is a process that builds over time. Small loving acts are like little steps that stimulate self-love. I consider faith to be the glue—the power tool for building self-love and becoming an empowered person. Become more conscious of where your thoughts go when you have a problem. Try using faith for small issues and as you see it works, try more. The more you see faith work, the more you'll trust it. The more you try and have a positive outcome, the more you'll be motivated to use faith as a tool for getting through life in a happier and relaxed way.

You get as much as your mind allows. If you believe you can, you can. The contrary is true too. Be careful not to attract negatives.

Faith is a real gift of love to you. I implore you to use it if you want a happier life!

DAY 18 ASSIGNMENT

Be patient with yourself.

Let go of urgency and fear. Relax and transform striving into thriving. Trust in yourself, do good work, and you will see results.

DAY 18 AFFIRMATION

I choose faith over fear!

Day 19

Take A Break

From Stress

It doesn't matter what the world throws at you. Things at work may be nuts. Your spouse is driving you crazy. Your kids are getting into trouble. The weather is miserable. Family members demanding your attention and calling you all day long.

Do you let all these things affect your mood and perspective of how good life really is?

Unless you consciously choose a different direction, stress will beat you up!

Allowing stress to go unchecked is very unloving to you! Doing something to relieve it, even temporarily, says, "I love me!" Find things that make you happy and focus on them instead of on problems.

Find something that reduces your stress and do it regularly. Give yourself the gift of a more relaxed you. It's your choice. Let stress control you or you take control of the stress, so it doesn't take over your life. Less stress leaves more room to be happy, and feel self-love.

DAY 19 ASSIGNMENT

Don't participate in activities that bring you down. Don't allow toxic people in your life. Love everyone, but be discerning on who you allow into your life.

- Make a list of activities that bring you down.
- Write down ways that these activities can be eliminated from your life
- Make a list of the toxic people in y our life.
- Write down ways in which you can limit your amount of time spent with these people.

DAY 19 AFFIRMATION

I give myself the gift of relaxation
every day

Day 20

List Your

Blessings

Can you believe that we are already on day 20? The time has literally flown by.

Here is your day 20 self-love message.

You've probably heard it many times, but that's because it's true. If you want to love yourself, focus on your blessings. Write down the things that make you smile or that you feel good about having. Then read each one out loud, starting with, "I'm grateful for_____." The more you appreciate your blessings, the better you feel. The better you feel, the more you'll fall in love with you.

Studies show that people who practice gratitude are healthier, happier, more productive, and earn more money than those who are not appreciative of what they already have. People with gratitude tend to have stronger relationships with friends, family, coworkers, and partners. An attitude of gratitude boosts careers, allows us to more easily overcome challenges, resolve problems, and manage stress.

Count your blessings every day. Add to your list whenever you can. Look for things to be grateful for. It will help you appreciate your life more!

Day 20 Assignment

Create a gratitude journal: Each night before you go to bed write down 3 things that you are thankful for.

DAY 20 AFFIRMATION

I appreciate and show gratitude for all of my blessings!

Day 21

Get Up, Dress Up, And Show Up!

Well! Today is the last day of our 21 Days of Self--Love. I hope that it was beneficial and helped you to develop the habit of loving yourself more. Just because the challenge is over, does not mean that you stop showing yourself love on a daily basis. Remember to make a commitment to yourself to do something loving every single day, no matter how big or small. Just one small act of self-love per day can make a huge difference in how your day goes.

DAY 21 ASSIGNMENT

Get Up, Dress Up, and Show Up!

No matter how you feel, Get up, dress up, and show up! Celebrate yourself by dressing up, even if you work from home. Make tomorrow your day! Wear your favorite outfit, a fancy scarf, a special dress, and high heels. Wear the jewelry you only wear on really special occasions. If anyone asks why you dressed up, tell them because you want to and that you are celebrating yourself! Have fun with it!

Remember...When you look good, you feel good!

DAY 21 AFFIRMATION

I am well groomed, healthy and full of confidence. My outer well-being is matched by my inner wellbeing.

Bonus

Assignment

Write a love letter to yourself.

Instead of focusing on the negatives, only write down the positive things about yourself! Write why you're proud of who you are, why you're beautiful and traits that you love. Dig deep and tell yourself all the things you wish someone had told you. Think about how you made it out of those tough situations or how you learned to fight through your struggles.

Add gratitude, appreciation, and love to yourself about yourself. Take some time, put some conscious and generous thoughts and feelings into it and allow yourself to boldly express your love for yourself.

When you are finished, fold the letter and place it in the envelope, seal it, and address it to yourself. Put the stamp on and, when you have a chance, drop it in a mailbox. When the letter arrives, take a few minutes when you know you won't be disturbed, find a private place, and read the letter carefully.

You may find that you are moved to tears by it; allow your feelings to flow. Thank your inner spirit for understanding you so well. Refold the letter and put it back in its envelope, and keep it where you can reread it and take its message of love to heart whenever you have the need.

yourself

The Top 5 Benefits of Self-Love

1. You don't "need" anyone to make you happy.

2. You effortlessly become or maintain your ideal weight.

3. You attract friends and lovers who truly love you & bring you joy.

4. You attract & manifest what you desire with ease and elegance.

5. You are able to make a real impact as you serve your purpose on earth.

Of course, there are many, many more benefits of self-love, but these are at the top of my list.

Love yourself enough to take
the actions required for
your happiness.

A Message From The Author

Thank you for taking the self-love journey. I hope that it was beneficial and helped you to develop the habit of loving yourself more. Just because the 21 days are over, does not mean that you stop showing yourself love. Continue to make a commitment to yourself to do something loving every single day, no matter how big or small. Just one small act of self-love per day is guaranteed to make a huge difference in your life.

Love yourself enough to believe in the limitless opportunities available to you. Take action and create a beautiful life for yourself.

Tamiko

The greatest love affair you will ever have in your life is the one you have with yourself.

About The Author

Tamiko Lowry-Pugh, often referred to as "The Empowering Diva" is a voice for Women's Empowerment. As the CEO of EmpowerME! Life Coaching & Consulting, and The founder of The Still Standing Foundation, she has constructed a powerful movement dedicated to the empowerment and personal development of women across the world. She is a compassionate mentor and friend, an enthusiastic leader, and visionary. As an International Bestselling Author, Inspirational Speaker,

Empowerment Specialist, and Domestic Violence Educator, Tamiko believes that empowerment comes from within and can be achieved by honoring yourself, your values, and expressing your talents and gifts. www.tamikolowry.com

Made in the USA
Columbia, SC
30 December 2018